M000279112

Penguin Functional English

PAIR WORK

Activities for Effective Communication   *Student B*

Peter Watcyn-Jones

PENGUIN
ENGLISH

PENGUIN ENGLISH

Published by the Penguin Group
Penguin Books Ltd, 27 Wrights Lane, London W8 5TZ, England
Penguin Books USA Inc., 375 Hudson Street, New York, NY 10014, USA
Penguin Books Australia Ltd, Ringwood, Victoria, Australia
Penguin Books Canada Ltd, 10 Alcorn Avenue, Toronto, Ontario, Canada M4V 3B2
Penguin Books (NZ) Ltd, 182–90 Wairau Road, Auckland 10, New Zealand

Penguin Books Ltd, Registered Offices: Harmondsworth, Middlesex, England

First published 1981

20 19 18 17 16 15 14 13 12 11

Copyright © Peter Watcyn-Jones, 1981
All rights reserved

Printed and bound in Great Britain by
BPC Hazell Books Ltd
A member of
The British Printing Company Ltd

Except in the United States of America, this book is sold subject
to the condition that it shall not, by way of trade or otherwise, be lent,
re-sold, hired out, or otherwise circulated without the publisher's
prior consent in any form of binding or cover other than that in
which it is published and without a similar condition including this
condition being imposed on the subsequent purchaser

ISBN 0 14 081 321 7
Pair Work A Student A ISBN 0 14 081 320 9

Contents

Acknowledgements

The author and publishers wish to thank the following
for the use of copyright material in this book: British
Tourist Authority for p. 15; Courtaulds Limited for p. 35;
Greater London Council Photograph Library for p. 33;
Pilgrims Publications Canterbury and Carlos Maeztu
for allowing us to base Unit 1 on 'From a Humanistic
Education Workshop led by Howard Kirshenbaum' taken
from the book *Recipe Book for Tired Teachers – No 1*
under the title 'Dynamic Encounter'.

To the teacher

Pair Work forms part of the Penguin Functional English course and was written to give classes, working in pairs, further practice in the functions introduced in *Impact* and *Dialogues*. Unlike most courses, *Pair Work* consists of two books, one for Student A and the other for Student B. There are two basic reasons for this:

1 In most language situations there is always an element of the unexpected – of not knowing exactly what the person you are talking to is going to say, even though on some occasions you may have a general idea (e.g. when ordering food in a restaurant). Unfortunately, most books give little practice in this since all too often every student has access to the same material as everyone else in the class with the result that anything that is said is often predictable. This, in turn, gives the students a false sense of security, so that once the whole context or the set-piece is removed they often find difficulty in communicating outside the classroom. *Pair Work* tries to overcome this by making sure from the beginning that Student A does not have access to Student B's information, and vice versa. In this way students are forced to react with one another and to respond to the unexpected – which is, after all, an essential requirement for true communication.

2 Another important aspect of language learning which again is often neglected is training students to listen effectively. Whereas listening comprehension exercises are an attempt to overcome this problem they are, in most cases, fairly passive activities and all too often removed from reality. Instead, what we should be concentrating on is in students listening effectively to one another. Again, when all the information is available to everyone in the class such intensive listening is not necessary since the student can always read anything he or she does not understand. But by removing what the other speaker is going to say the student is immediately forced into a situation where he or she not only has to but wants to listen intensively in order to be able to talk to the other person – which is, after all, the situation he or she is going to be in when he or she leaves the comparative safety of the classroom.

Description of the material

Each book contains forty activities. These are arranged, where possible, into pairs of activities so that if Student A has one particular role or task in the first activity then he or she has Student B's role or task in the second, and vice versa. This gives both students practice in the same function but avoids the possibly boring alternative of simply changing parts and doing exactly the same activity again. Instead of this, the same function is practised again but the situation (or role) is changed. (See Note 1, page 7)

There are five main types of activities in the books:

1 **Role-plays**
These are activities in which students are given definite roles to play and are usually asked to assume a different name, background, age, etc. (See Note 2)

An example of a role-play is Activity 17 – Newspaper interviews.

2 **Simulation exercises**
These are activities in which students can play themselves but are given a definite task to do or are put in a specific situation and asked to make appropriate responses.

An example of a simulation exercise is Activity 8 – Asking for train information.

3 **One-sided dialogues**
These are activities in which students read a dialogue together but can only see their own part, which usually includes opportunities for the student to make his or her own responses.

An example of a one-sided dialogue is Activity 10 – At a restaurant.

4 **Information-gap activities**
These are activities in which students are asked to perform a task together; they fall into two types. In the first, one student has access to all the information and tries to impart it to his or her partner.

An example of this type is Activity 15 – Complete the drawing (1). In the second, both students are given access to half the information and by working together try to solve the whole.

An example of this type is Activity 13 – Fill in the missing information (1).

5 **Discussion and conversation activities**
These are activities designed to stimulate students to discuss a subject or subjects with their partner and usually take the form of a questionnaire. These activities are particularly useful when students are practising giving opinions and showing agreement or disagreement.

An example of a discussion or conversation activity is Activity 14 – Children and parents.

How to use the books

Since the activities have been written to give extra practice in certain functions they are best done as follow-up work since the books assume that the student has a basic mastery of the language needed to perform the various functions. Again, although specifically written to supplement *Impact* and *Dialogues* there is no reason why the books cannot be used with any other existing functionally based course at intermediate level or above.

A list of functions is given on page 8 with the number of the activity or activities which practise them. All the teacher has to do is decide which function needs practising and choose an appropriate activity from the ones given. Since, in some instances, more than one activity has been written to practise a particular function, repeated practice can be given without the students becoming bored. Since the level throughout the book is intermediate there is no need to take the activities in order if the needs of the class dictate otherwise. Indeed, it is not envisaged that the book should be worked through from beginning to end: the activities can, and should, be taken in any order depending on the needs of any particular class.

Teaching hints

1 Clear instructions are given for all the activities so that all the teacher has to do is ask the students to turn to a particular activity and let them read through the instructions. While the students do this, the teacher can go around the class checking that they have fully understood what they have to do before starting. When the students are ready they begin. It is better if all the pairs start working at the same time, rather than working one after the other.

2 Before starting, the room should be arranged in such a way that pairs face one another across a desk or table. This is to give them 'eye-contact' which makes communication a lot easier. Again, if possible, a bag or some sort of screen should be placed between them so that they cannot see one another's books.

3 Since the students will be working in pairs, the pairs should be changed as often as possible so that students get a chance to work with (and get to know) different people in the class.

4 Should the group be made up of an odd number of students, then the teacher may be forced into working with one of the students. If this is nearly always the case, the teacher should choose a different student to work with each time. However, if a teacher feels reluctant to join in there is no reason why one of the students couldn't act as a passive observer and sit and listen to one of the pairs – noting, if possible, any mistakes which are made and commenting afterwards on the pair's performance. The student could then exchange roles with one of the more confident students, so that at least one role is taken by every student in the class.

5 During an activity the teacher moves from pair to pair, as a passive observer, noting problems or mistakes which can be taken up with the whole group after the activity has finished. In fact, it is always a good idea to spend a few minutes discussing the activity afterwards.

6 It is a good idea occasionally after a group has done a particular activity to ask one of the pairs to carry out the activity while the rest of the group listen and comment on their performance.

7 The length of the activities varies from approximately five to twenty minutes although, if the group is a particularly imaginative one, some of them (especially the role-plays) could take longer. It is up to the teacher and group to decide whether to spend a whole lesson on the activities or else to make them a part of a normal lesson. (Perhaps a combination of these two is a good idea.)

8 Although Activities 1 and 2 give practice in asking and answering personal questions, the chief reason for putting them first in the book is that they are a useful way of breaking the ice when the group is a new one – although they are still useful when the group has been together for some time. However, if the group includes students who are sensitive about giving personal information about themselves, the teacher can tell them not to answer any question which they may not wish to answer; they can simply say they cannot think of anything in reply to these questions.

9 Not all activities are appropriate for all classes. Any which are not can simply be omitted (for example, Activity 14 may not be acceptable in all cultures).

Notes

1 Of course, if the teacher and group would like to repeat activities, then there is no reason why students couldn't change books and do them again. This can be done at a later date.

2 For more detailed notes on role-play as well as further examples, see another book by Peter Watcyn-Jones, *Act English* (also published by Penguin Books Ltd).

Guide to functions practised

Function	Number of activity
Asking and answering personal questions	1, 2
Asking and answering questions about likes and dislikes	3
Asking and answering questions about future plans	4, 13
Asking about and stating wants and needs	5, 6, 10, 11, 12, 31, 32
Giving advice	7 (dialogue 1)
Passing on and reacting to a piece of news	7 (dialogue 2)
Apologies and excuses	7 (dialogues 3, 4), 26 (situations 1, 2)
Giving opinions/agreeing and disagreeing with an opinion	14, 19
Giving and receiving instructions	15, 16, 24, 25
Asking for and giving information	8, 9, (13), 33, 34, 37
Asking and answering questions	17, 18, 20, 21, 27, 29, 35, 38
Asking for and making suggestions	22
Socializing	26 (situation 3), 28
Asking for and giving directions	23
Asking for help	26 (situation 4)
Talking about degrees of certainty/uncertainty	30
Inviting and making arrangements	36
Two 'sort it out' activities	39, 40

Getting to know one another

Read the sentences below and write down your answers on the following page.

Look at the top left-hand corner of the next page:

Next to number 1, write down the name of the most beautiful area or town in your country.

Next to number 2, write down the year you started learning English.

Next to number 3, write down who you would be if you could be any person in the world (someone who is still alive).

In the circle under number 3, write down the first name of the first girl or boy you were attracted to (or fell in love with)!

Look at the bottom right-hand corner:

Next to number 4, write down the first name of your favourite teacher at school.

Next to number 5, write down something that once made you very frightened.

Next to number 6, write down something that you really love doing.

In the circle above number 4, write down the first name of your favourite uncle or aunt.

Look at the top right-hand corner:

In the rectangle, write down the name of the town or village where you were born.

In the circle underneath, write down what you consider to be the ideal age to get married.

Look at the bottom left-hand corner:

In the rectangle, write down the name of your favourite composer, pop singer or pop group.

In the circle above, write down how old you were when you came closest to dying (e.g. through illness or an accident).

Look at the large rectangle in the middle of the page:

Write your first name in the rectangle in LARGE LETTERS.

In the blank spaces around it write down three things you hate doing.

When you have finished, change books with Student A. Look at what he or she has written and ask him or her as many questions as you can about it, e.g. What does this date here mean? Who is this person? etc. Try to get him or her to talk as much as possible about each thing. (Of course, you will also be expected to talk about what you have written!)

1 _____

2 _____

3 _____

4 _____

5 _____

6 _____

Read through the sentences below, then put a circle around the number which most closely coincides with the way you usually behave. Before starting, look at the Key.

I find it easy to get out of bed in the mornings.	1	2	3	4	5
I watch at least one T.V. programme or listen to at least one radio programme in the evenings.	1	2	3	4	5
I feel nervous when meeting new people.	1	2	3	4	5
I am good with money.	1	2	3	4	5
I feel bored when I am alone.	1	2	3	4	5
I would rather be with members of the opposite sex than with members of my own sex.	1	2	3	4	5
I try to keep up with the latest world news.	1	2	3	4	5
I get annoyed if people are late.	1	2	3	4	5
I prefer going out at weekends to staying at home.	1	2	3	4	5
I think things over carefully before making a decision.	1	2	3	4	5
I try to make at least one or two new friends every year.	1	2	3	4	5
I go abroad in the summer.	1	2	3	4	5
I remember people's names when I am introduced to them.	1	2	3	4	5
I plan for the future.	1	2	3	4	5
I find it easy to learn English.	1	2	3	4	5

KEY

1 Yes, always
2 Yes, usually
3 Well, it depends
4 No, not usually
5 No, never

When you have finished, compare your answers with Student A. Try to discuss each point – giving reasons why you do or don't do something.

3   Market research — television or radio programmes

Student A works for a Market Research Bureau. He/she is going to ask you questions about the types of television or radio programmes you watch or listen to. Answer his/her questions.

Before starting, here are some of the most common types of programmes on television or radio:

the news	serials
films or discussion programmes	plays
quiz shows	detective series
pop music programmes	chat shows
comedy programmes	children's programmes
documentaries	variety shows
classical music programmes	sports programmes

4   Holiday survey

Your class at school are doing a survey on how people spend their summer holidays. You are going to interview people in the street about their holiday plans and write down their answers on the Holiday Survey Sheet on the opposite page. Student A is a passer-by.

Before starting, study the Holiday Survey Sheet and work out questions to ask. For example:

Where are you going for your holiday this year?
When are you going?
How long are you planning to stay there?
How are you getting there?   etc.

You can begin like this:

Excuse me, I'm doing a survey on how people spend their summer holidays. Would you mind if I asked you a few questions?

And finish:

Thank you very much for answering my questions.

HOLIDAY SURVEY SHEET

1 Place/country: ....

2 Date of holiday: ....

3 Length of stay: ....

4 Is it a charter holiday?   Yes/No

5 Travel arrangements: by air ... by car ... by boat ...

    by bus ... by train ... Any other: ....

6 Accommodation: hotel ... guest house ... country inn ...

    motel ... youth hostel ... caravan ... tent ... Any other?: ......

7 What are you hoping to do there?

    go swimming ... go fishing ... go dancing ... play golf ...

    go sightseeing ... visit museums ... go for walks ...

    go shopping ... Anything else: ....

8 Who are you going with? ....

9 Cost of holiday: £ ....

10 Reason for choosing this particular holiday:

    ....

    ....

Booking a room at a hotel (1)

THE SURREY HOTEL
Cornfield Terrace
Southbourne
Tel: (0223) 927681

* ✳ 10 mins from Southbourne station
* ✳ 45 bedrooms – 25 with private bathroom
* ✳ Central heating throughout
  (No air-conditioning)
* ✳ Lift to all floors
* ✳ Large bar and restaurant
* ✳ Weekend entertainment
* ✳ Children welcome – and dogs too!
* ✳ Night porter
* ✳ T.V. lounge
* ✳ Private car park
* ✳ 5 mins from shops and beach

CHARGES PER NIGHT – BED AND BREAKFAST

Single room £45.50
Single room with bath £50.00
Twin/double room £60.50
Twin/double room with bath £65.00

You are a receptionist at the hotel shown on the opposite page. Student A phones up to make a reservation.

Before starting, have a pen or pencil ready to write down all the necessary information. Make sure you get the following:

---

1 The person's name (you may have to ask him/her to spell it).
2 The type of room required (e.g. single, double, etc.).
3 The day/date of arrival.
4 Length of stay.

You can also include other details about the hotel, e.g. if it has a restaurant, T.V. lounge, etc.

Here is a form you can use when writing down the necessary information:

Name: ....

Accommodation: ....

Date of arrival: ....

Length of stay: ....

Other details: ....

....

You can begin like this:

Good (*morning*). Surrey Hotel.

6   Booking a room at a hotel (2)

```
★★ ♨ Longton House GL7 2LE ☎73836
Situated ¾ mile outside town on Gloucester Road.
Jacobean and Georgian manor house delightfully
furnished with antiques and with a display of
antique pottery. Terrace and walled garden.
Open all year; Licensed: 30rm(16⇆) 🏧
ColourTV 90P 3🏠 (30p) English & Continental
Last dinner 10pm

★★Monarch Seafront Parade, CO15 1PU
☎321215
Victorian building with modern interior;
overlooking sea.
```

You have decided to take your two children to Dackton for a few days. Phone up the Monarch Hotel and make a reservation.

You want to stay for five nights and would like a twin room with bath, plus an extra bed in the same room, if possible. You would also like a room overlooking the sea.

You will be driving down to Dackton the day after tomorrow and want to know if the hotel is difficult to find.

Your children love watching T.V. and you would like to have one in your room.

Student A is the hotel receptionist.

You can begin like this:

> Good (*morning*). My name's (*Janet Smith*). I'd like to book a room at your hotel for five nights.

7   Carrying on a conversation

Opposite are the opening words of four dialogues. Working with Student A, try to make the conversation go on for as long as possible. Before starting, think for a few minutes about what it might be possible to say. (But do *not* discuss the dialogue with Student A!) When you are both ready, begin the conversation.

Dialogue 1
You play the part of B. Student A plays the part of A.

> A: You look upset,...... (*say person's name*).
> What's wrong?
> B: Oh, it's just that...... (*carry on the conversation*).

Dialogue 2
You play the part of A. Student A plays the part of B.

> A: It's a pity about John, isn't it?
> B: John? What do you mean?
> A: Well, haven't you heard?
> B: Heard what?
> A: ...... (*carry on the conversation*).

Dialogue 3
You play the part of B. Student A plays the part of A.

> A: 978574.
> B: Hello. Is that...... (*say person's name*)?
> A: Yes.
> B: It's...... (*say your name*). Where on earth were you last
> night?
> A: Last night?...... (*carry on the conversation*).

Dialogue 4
You play the part of A. Student A plays the part of B.

> A: Excuse me, is that your dog over there?
> B: Yes, that's right.
> A: Well, it's just bitten my friend!
> B: ...... (*carry on the conversation*).

8   Asking for train information

You are a clerk at the Central Station in Paris. Student A phones you up for some information about trains to and from Madrid.

Answer his/her inquiries with the help of the time-tables below.

Time-table PARIS – BURGOS – MADRID					Daily
Paris . . . . .dep.	18.02	22.49	00.09	06.45	13.56
Burgos . . . . .arr.	05.24	11.49	16.49	18.48	02.59
dep.	05.29	11.53	17.01	18.52	03.04
Madrid (Charmartin) arr.	09.00	14.45	21.04	21.50	08.30

Time-table MADRID – BURGOS – PARIS					Daily
Madrid (Charmartin) dep.	22.05	07.55	12.40	15.45	19.00
Burgos . . . . .arr.	03.05	10.47	16.27	18.38	22.08
dep.	03.08	10.51	16.37	18.42	22.10
Paris .arr.	16.19	23.35	07.50	07.50	09.35

9   Asking for boat information

You live in England. Your sister teaches in Gothenburg in Sweden and has invited you to spend two weeks with her in July. You phone up the Fjord Line to find out about boats to Sweden. You want to arrive in Gothenburg on or about 12 July.

Student A is a clerk for the Fjord Line.

Before starting, have a pen ready to make a note of the following:

Date of departure from Felixstowe	....
Time of departure from Felixstowe	....
Date of arrival in Gothenburg	....
Time of arrival in Gothenburg	....
Cost (a) Fare	....
(b) Berth	....

You can begin like this:

Good (*morning*). I'd like some information about boats to Gothenburg.

10   One-sided dialogue: at a restaurant

Read the following dialogue with Student A.

Unfortunately, you can only see your part, so you will have to listen very carefully to what Student A says. Use the menu on the next page.

Before starting, read through your part to get an idea of what the dialogue is all about.

Student A: ......

        Yes: Yes, very nice indeed. You come here often, then?

Student A: ......

        You: Oh no! I've only been here once before, actually. That was...... (*say when it was*).

Student A: ......

        You: Well, I wouldn't mind...... (*name a dish*). What about you?

Student A: ......

        You: Right. And what shall we have for the main course? The ...... (*name a dish*) sounds rather nice.

Student A: ......

        You: Oh, in that case, I'll have...... (*repeat the dish*) too.

Student A: ......

        You: Well, let's see what's on the menu.

Student A: ......

        You: Yes . . . that sounds good for me as well. I'll order the same.

Student A: ......

<u>THE INN PLACE</u>

<u>TABLE D'HOTE DINNER MENU</u>

£21.50

Iced Melon	Grapefruit Cocktail
Avocado Pear	Pâté Maison
Prawn Cocktail	Various Soups

Grilled Halibut with Lemon
Baked Plaice and Mushrooms
Veal Escalope
Minute Steak Garni
Lamb and Mushroom Ragoût
Roast Turkey with Rosemary Butter Stuffing
Chicken and Bacon Pie
Rice and Mushroom Salad
Cold Meat Salads (Various)

Chips	Soufflé Potatoes	Garden Peas
New Potatoes	Carrots	French Beans
Tomatoes	Mushrooms	Cauliflower

Fruit Salad	Various Ice Creams
Apple Pie	Cheese and Biscuits

Coffee and Drinks Extra

Service Charge Included

Looking for a house/flat (1)

HOUSES, FLATS, etc.
*Various properties
to be let*

NORTH WALES. Welsh Farm-
house to let. Fabulous countryside, available July – September.
Phone: Bangor 7422.

GIRL WANTED to share mixed
house in Kensington.
Phone: 071-579 4607

You are looking for a house to rent during August. It is for you and two other friends of yours. You would like a house somewhere away from towns and cities – preferably in Wales or Scotland – because you are hoping to write a play together. You are also hoping to do some fishing. It must be fairly modern and have at least two bedrooms. You would also like a telephone. You are prepared to pay up to £400 for the month.

You see the above advertisement in the newspaper and decide to phone up about it. Student A is the person who owns the farmhouse.

You can begin like this:

Good (*morning*). I'm phoning about the farmhouse to let.

(Note: If you are interested, you may want to arrange a time to see the house.)

Looking for a house/flat (2)

You want to let your flat in Chelsea. It is a large, luxury one and has four bedrooms, a large sitting/dining room and a modern kitchen. You also share the garden and there is plenty of parking space outside the house. The rent is £700 a month. The flat is available now. The address is 44 Chelsea Square, and the flat can be viewed any evening after 6 p.m. or at weekends.

You have put an advertisement in the newspaper about it. Student A is going to phone you up for further details.

13   Fill in the missing information (1)

By asking Student A questions, fill in the missing information in the table on the opposite page. (Student A will also ask you questions.)

Before starting, work out the type of questions you will need to ask. For example:

Who is arriving on ... (*say date*)?
What nationality is ... (*say name*)?
When is ... (*say name*) ... arriving at the conference?
How long is ... (*say name*) ... staying?
At which hotel is ... (*say name*) ... staying?
At what time is ... (*say name*) ... giving a lecture?
On what date is the lecture on ... (*say subject*)?
etc.

When you have both finished, compare your tables to check that you have filled in the missing information correctly.

(Note: If, in answer to one of your questions, Student A says he/she doesn't know the answer, then try another sort of question to get the same information, since it may be that Student A has not yet filled in the information you based your first question on.)

List and details of participants

	Name	Nationality	Date of arrival	Length of stay	Hotel
1	Janet Hoover	American	5 June	a fortnight	The Hilton
2	Sven Borg	Swedish	3 June	10 days	
3			7 June	4 days	The Winston Churchill
4	Brigitte Dubois	French	6 June	a week	The Dorchester
5		German		5 days	Royal Kensington
6	Sir Roger Bloom	English	5 June		
7	Viktor Pavlova	Russian	3 June	8	Cen

	Date and time of lecture		Subject of lecture
1			In Search of UFOs
2	8 June	9.30 a.m.	
3	9 June	3.15 p.m.	E.S.P. – The Sixth Sense?
4	11 June		
5	12 June	1.30 p.m.	The Mystery of Atlantis
6	6 June	10.15 a.m.	The Secret Life of Plants
7	15 June		The Great Tele

14 Questionnaire: children and parents

Read through the sentences below, then put a circle around the number which most closely coincides with your opinion. Before starting, look at the Key.

KEY	
1	Yes, definitely
2	Yes, perhaps
3	Well, that depends
4	No, not really
5	No, definitely not

Children should obey their parents without question.	1 2 3 4 5
It is an advantage to be an only child.	1 2 3 4 5
Girls and boys should be brought up in the same way – without definite roles.	1 2 3 4 5
Most men would prefer to have a son as their first child.	1 2 3 4 5
You should never hit a child.	1 2 3 4 5
It is a child's duty to look after his or her parents when they are old.	1 2 3 4 5
Parents should never quarrel in front of their children.	1 2 3 4 5
The best way of punishing a child is to stop his or her pocket money.	1 2 3 4 5
Babies are boring.	1 2 3 4 5
It is wrong for both parents to go out to work if they have small children.	1 2 3 4 5
No family should be allowed to have more than four children nowadays.	1 2 3 4 5
Children under 18 should never be out later than 11 o'clock in the evening.	1 2 3 4 5

When you have finished, discuss your answers with Student A.
Remember to give reasons for your opinion – and even to argue with what Student A says if you disagree with him or her.

Complete the drawing (1)

Below is an incomplete map of Black Island. Student A has a completed version. He/she is going to help you complete yours.

You are allowed to ask questions but you must not look at Student A's map.

When you have finished, compare maps.

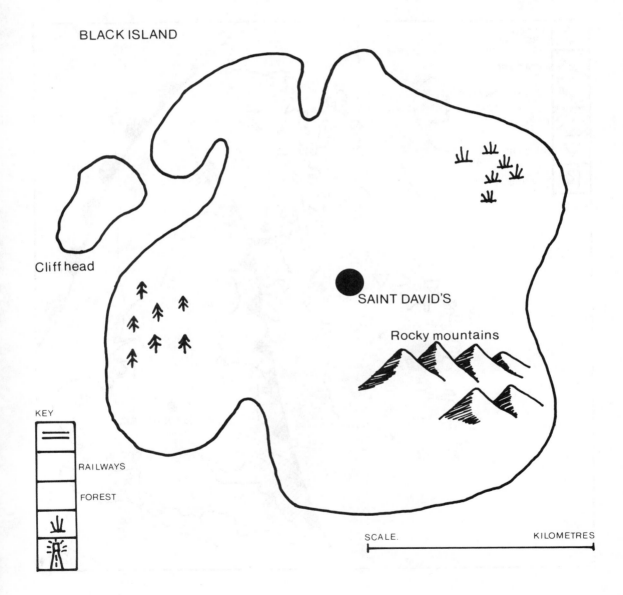

16   Complete the drawing (2)

Student A has an incomplete drawing of the weather map of Great Britain.

Help him/her complete it by telling him/her what to draw and answering his/her questions. But you must not touch his/her map or let him/her see yours.

When you have finished, compare your drawings.

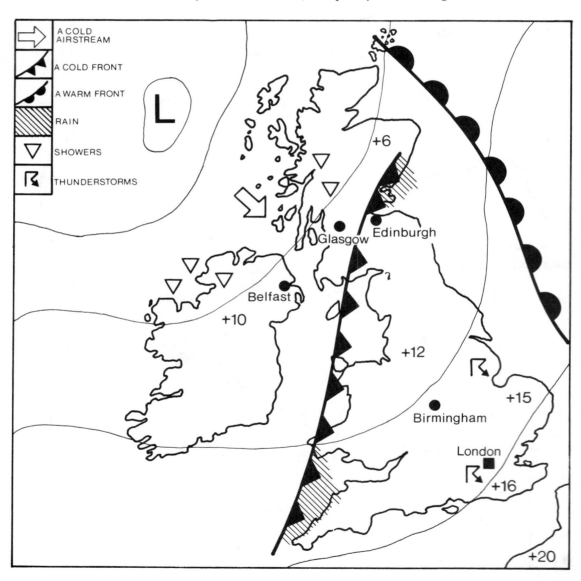

Newspaper interviews (1)

Your name is Albert Sykes/Anita Sykes.

Until a few weeks ago you worked as a gardener for the famous detective-story writer, Anthea Crystal (Arthur Crystal). Then, to everyone's surprise, you got married. You started working for your wife (husband) thirty years ago. He/she was a wonderful person and was always very kind and interested in what you were doing. But it was only in the past year that your relationship became a romantic one You always felt attracted to Anthea (Arthur) but had no idea that he/she thought of you as anything but a gardener. It was he/she who suggested getting married. You spent your honeymoon in Iceland which was where Anthea's (Arthur's) first novel – *Seven Big Vikings* – was set. You are going to carry on being a gardener.

You have agreed to be interviewed by a reporter from the *Daily Mirror*. Student A is the reporter.

When you answer his/her questions, try to use your own words as much as possible.

You are a reporter for the magazine *The Cinema Today*. You are going to interview the film director Antonio Arpeggio/Antonia Arpeggio, whose latest film, *Lucky*, recently won five Oscars, including the 'Best picture of the year' and 'Best director' awards. The film, also written by Arpeggio, only cost $300,000 to make. No one thought it would be a success and most of the major film companies turned it down.

Before starting, work out some questions to ask. For example:

> When did you first get the idea for the film?
> When did you write it?
> Why wouldn't the major film companies take it on?
> What is the story about?
> Why do people like it, do you think?
> etc.

You can begin like this:

> How do you do, Mr/Miss Arpeggio. I'm (*Pamela Brown*) from *The Cinema Today*. It was kind of you to let me interview you.

Read through the sentences below, then put a circle around the number which most closely coincides with your opinion. Before starting, look at the Key.

		KEY
There is no life after death.	1 2 3 4 5	**1** I agree entirely
Wars never solve anything.	1 2 3 4 5	**2** I agree on the whole
We should try to cure criminals, not punish them.	1 2 3 4 5	**3** I can't make up my mind
People suffering from incurable diseases should be painlessly put to death if they request it.	1 2 3 4 5	**4** I disagree on the whole
Men and women can never be equal.	1 2 3 4 5	**5** I disagree entirely
It is wrong to pay people so much money for playing sport.	1 2 3 4 5	
People should wait until they are at least 24 before getting married.	1 2 3 4 5	
People were a lot happier 'in the old days'.	1 2 3 4 5	
There is too much fuss made about nuclear power nowadays.	1 2 3 4 5	
Divorce is wrong.	1 2 3 4 5	
Most people keep pets because they are lonely or have difficulty in making relationships with other people.	1 2 3 4 5	
The United Nations is a waste of time and money.	1 2 3 4 5	

When you have finished, discuss your answers with Student A. Remember to give reasons for your opinion – and even to argue with Student A if you disagree with him or her.

Visiting a school

You are a teacher at Horam Primary School (that is, a school for children aged 7–11). It is your class in the photograph.

A foreign student (Student A) is visiting the school for the day and has just been shown into your classroom by the headmaster. He or she is going to ask you some questions about the school and the pupils.

Before starting, think about the following:

- the size of the school
- number of children per class
- number of teachers
- when school starts/finishes
- number of lessons per day
- age of children in your class
- what sort of pupils they are
- what subjects they like/dislike
    etc.

(Note: If you don't know the true answer to Student A's questions, use your imagination!)

Visiting a factory

You are a foreign student and have been invited to a local factory for the day. You have just arrived at this part of the factory.

Student A is the Works Manager who is showing you around and you are going to ask him/her questions about the factory and the people who work there. For instance:

> What are these people doing?
> Do they work in shifts?
> How many people work at the factory altogether?
> How many of them are women?
> How much do they get paid for doing this?
> Does the factory export much?
> etc.

Look at the photograph and try to think of other questions. (You may even want to ask questions about some of the people or machines in the photograph.)

When you have finished, you can say:

> Thank you very much for showing me around the factory. It's been really interesting.

22   One-sided dialogue: what shall we do this weekend?

Read the following dialogue with Student A.

You are friends and are talking about where to go at the weekend.

Unfortunately, you can only see your part of the dialogue, so you will have to listen very carefully to what Student A says. Use the *Weekend Guide* on the page opposite.

Before starting, read through your part to get an idea of what the dialogue is all about.

You:	Do you fancy doing something this weekend, ... (*say person's name*)?
Student A:	......
You:	Well ... something different. I'm a bit fed up with doing the same old thing every weekend.
Student A:	......
You:	I'm not sure, really.
Student A:	......
You:	Yes, there is, isn't there? (*look at Guide.*) Now, let's see ... Ah! This sounds interesting!
Student A:	......
You:	...... (*read something from OTHER EVENTS*)
Student A:	......
You:	All right. What about ...... (*make another suggestion from COACH TOURS*)
Student A:	......
You:	Well, what do you suggest, then?
Student A:	......
You:	...... (*repeat suggestion*). No, I can't say I fancy that. It doesn't sound very interesting.
Student A:	......
You:	Yes, that sounds better. What does it say about it?
Student A:	......
You:	Yes, that seems all right. Let's do that then, shall we?
Student A:	......
You:	Good. It'll be nice to do something different.

WEEKEND GUIDE

EXHIBITIONS

Women at War, 1914-1918
Photographic record. Public Library. Saturday 10–6.

Costumes Through the Ages
Costumes from the 16th century to today. Local Museum. Sat–Mon 10–4.30.

Model Railway Exhibition
Goldenhill Model Railway Club, St Andrew's Hall. Saturday 11–7. At least 16 working layouts on view.

SPORTING EVENTS

Tenpin Bowling
National Championships at The Bowl. All day Saturday and Sunday.

Charity Football Match
Charity football match between House of Commons team and Entertainers team at Pilot Fields. Saturday afternoon 2 p.m.

Stockcar Racing
International meeting at Burlight. Disco afterwards. Saturday afternoon 2.15 p.m.

COACH TOURS

Castle Howard, York
The most beautiful historic house in Yorkshire. Grounds, restaurant and cafeteria. House and Costume Gallery. Depart Saturday 8.30 a.m.

Kent Coastal Tour
See pleasant countryside of Kent as well as miles of coastline. Lunch at Dover. Depart Saturday 10 a.m.

Mystery Tour
Tour to somewhere famous. Details will not be given until you arrive. Depart Saturday 9 a.m.

OTHER EVENTS

Special Weekend for Railway Enthusiasts
Photographic weekend with special events including a 'Steam up' at Dackton Transport Museum. Saturday and Sunday 11 a.m.–5.30 p.m.

Antiques Fair
Opens on Saturday at Old Town Arts Centre. Saturday 11.30 a.m.–7.30 p.m. Admission £1.

Flower Power
Daffodil Festival at Otram. Two tons of bulbs already planted and a further 10,000 will decorate village. Saturday and Sunday.

Chess Championships
National chess championships on the Pier. Saturday–Tuesday 10.30 a.m.–7.30 p.m.

23   Asking for and giving directions

Take it in turns with Student A to ask for and give directions using the street plan on the opposite page.

You want directions for the following places (in this order):

FROM	TO
1 the station	the bank
2 the bank	the book shop
3 the book shop	the Grand Hotel
4 the Grand Hotel	the drugstore
5 the drugstore	the coffee bar

When Student A gives you directions, write the name (e.g. Bank) on the appropriate building.

The names of the buildings on the street plan opposite are the places Student A wants directions to. He/she is going to ask directions for the following places (in this order):

FROM	TO
1 the station	the police station
2 the police station	the boutique
3 the boutique	the post office
4 the post office	the museum
5 the museum	the restaurant

Ask for and give directions alternately. Student A starts. When you ask for directions, you can say:

Excuse me,	could you tell me the way to can you tell me how to get to	(the bank),	please?

When you have both finished, compare street plans to check that you have written the names of the various buildings in the correct places.

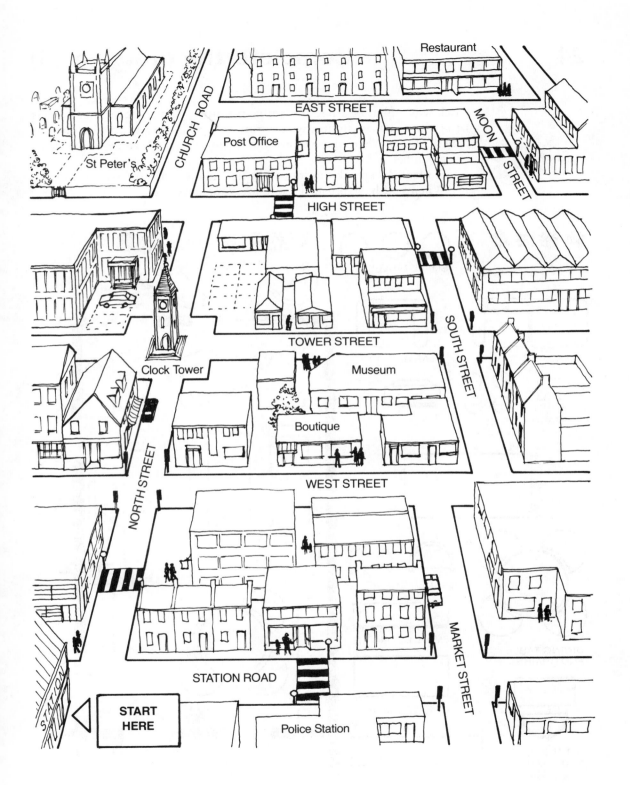

Below is a plan of a flat containing furniture, plants, etc. Student A has the same plan without any furniture. Help him/her to furnish the flat by telling him/her where to put the various items. (A guide to the items is given below.)

Student A can ask questions but he/she must not see your drawing. When you have finished, compare your drawings.

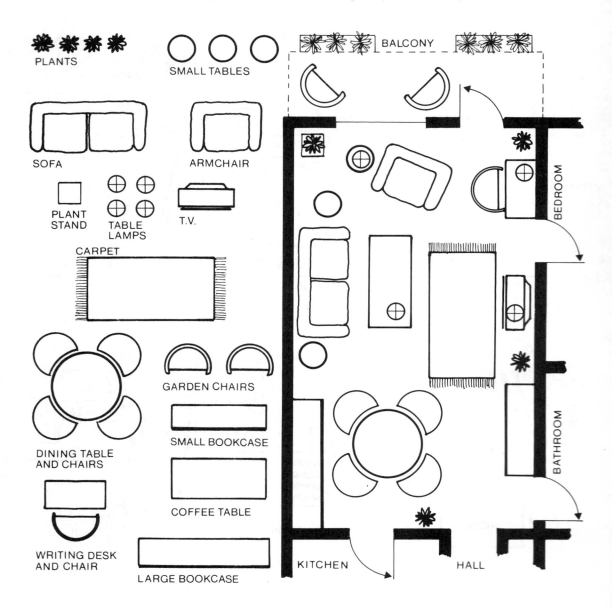

PLANTS

SMALL TABLES

BALCONY

SOFA

ARMCHAIR

PLANT STAND

TABLE LAMPS

T.V.

BEDROOM

CARPET

GARDEN CHAIRS

DINING TABLE AND CHAIRS

SMALL BOOKCASE

BATHROOM

COFFEE TABLE

WRITING DESK AND CHAIR

LARGE BOOKCASE

KITCHEN

HALL

Complete the drawing (4)

25

Below is a drawing of a kitchen. Student A has the same drawing but his/hers contains a number of objects (e.g. glasses, bottles, etc.). He/she is going to help you fill up your kitchen by telling you what to draw and where to put it. (A guide to the various objects to be drawn is given below.)

You are allowed to ask questions but you must not look at Student A's drawing. When you have finished, compare drawings.

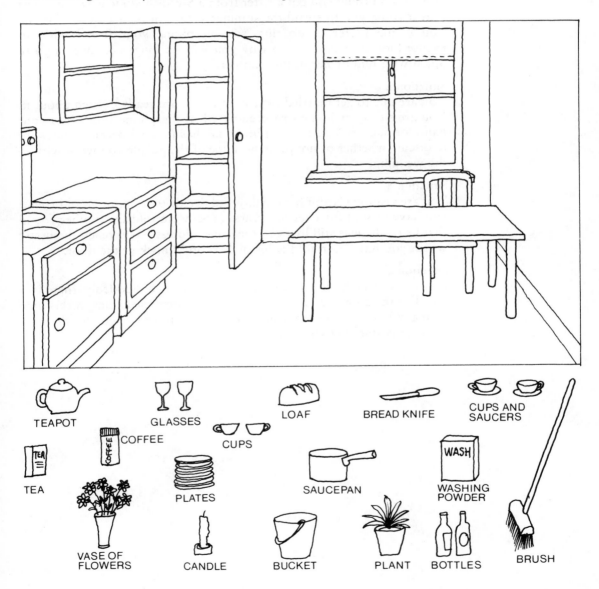

TEAPOT   GLASSES   LOAF   BREAD KNIFE   CUPS AND SAUCERS

COFFEE   CUPS

TEA   PLATES   SAUCEPAN   WASHING POWDER

VASE OF FLOWERS   CANDLE   BUCKET   PLANT   BOTTLES   BRUSH

Situations

Below are four situations which you are going to act out with Student A. Before starting, read through the situations (especially number 1 and number 3) and think a little about what you will say.

When you are both ready, act out the situation.

Situation 1
You have promised to go to Spain with a friend in the summer. However, this morning you got a letter from a Swedish student you met last year inviting you to spend the summer with him or her in Stockholm. You would prefer to do this, so you phone your friend with an excuse (not the truth!) as to why you will no longer be able to go to Spain with him or her in the summer.

Situation 2
You are due to get married next month and are really excited about it. You are sitting at home one evening when the phone rings. It is your fiancé or fiancée. You are glad he or she has phoned because you want to discuss whether or not to invite some of the people you work with to the wedding.

Situation 3
You are visiting Cardiff for the day and decide to look up an old friend you haven't seen for over ten years. (You were told by another friend that he or she was still living at the same address.) You reach the house which you have been told is his or hers and knock at the door.

Situation 4
It is 12.15 at night and you have just gone to bed. Suddenly, there is a knock at the door. You are a bit annoyed at someone calling at this time of night but you put on your dressing-gown and open the door. A stranger is standing on the doorstep!

27 Fill in the missing information (2)

By asking Student A questions, fill in the missing information in the passage below in pencil. (Student A will also ask you questions.)

IMMIGRANT IN BRITAIN

Abraham Jacobs lives in . . . . with his wife and six children. But he is not English. He was born in Kingston and came to Britain in . . . . 1970 – mainly because it was impossible to get a job in Jamaica. He lived in . . . . with relatives when he first arrived, then moved to Wolverhampton, ... and Liverpool before finally moving to . . . . where he has been living since 1975.

He spoke English fairly well on arrival, so he did not bother to attend any special English courses. His English is . . . . now and since three of his children were born in Britain, English is the only language spoken at home.

He likes England, but thinks there are three main problems facing immigrants. To begin with, it is difficult to get . . . . Secondly, there is the problem of finding . . . . and finally, there is still a lot of colour prejudice in Britain. In fact his children are still considered to be foreigners, even though three of them were born in England.

He works as a . . . . but has very little contact with English people since 95 per cent of his workmates are West Indians. And even outside work, the only contact he has with English people are one or two he meets when he goes to the local club.

July 19—

When you have finished, compare books to check that you have filled in the missing information correctly.

44

Meeting an old friend

You are Claire (or Peter) Smith.

You are waiting for a train on the Underground when you meet an old friend, Roger (or Joanna) Morgan, whom you haven't seen since your wedding ten years ago. (He/she went abroad a few days after it.) He/she used to go to school with your husband, Bill (your wife, Rita) and also used to go out with Alison/Alistair who is Scottish. The last you heard the engagement was off and he/she was now engaged to a Spaniard.

When you last saw him/her, you used to go dancing a lot. Your father also used to own the antique shop you now look after. Stop and have a chat.

Before starting, read through the above so that you remember the details without having to look at them too closely. Also think about what has happened to you since you last met (e.g. Do you have children? Do you still go dancing? Where are you living? etc.).

When you are ready, you can begin. (Student A will speak first.) Here are some phrases you can use:

(a) the meeting:	(*Roger!*) I haven't seen you for ages. How are you?
(b) talking about appearance:	What's happened to your ... (*hair/beard* etc.)? You're looking well.
(c) asking questions:	Where are you living/working nowadays? Are you still engaged? Do you ever hear from Alison/Alistair? Why didn't you write? etc.
(d) taking leave:	Yes, I'd better be on my way, too.
(e) making arrangements:	Why not come round and see us one day next week?

Above all, be prepared to use your imagination!
Student A is Roger Morgan or Joanna Morgan.
Note that *Alison* is a Scottish girl's name.

After the holiday

Think of somewhere in your country that would be an ideal place to go on holiday. Now imagine you are English and have just spent two weeks in this place. You are travelling home by bus from London when you get into conversation with the person sitting next to you (Student A), and end up talking about your holiday.

Before starting, think about the following:

- where you went
- why you chose this place for a holiday
- how you travelled
- who you went with
- where you stayed
- how you spent your time
- who you met
- what sort of food you ate
- what the weather was like
- what souvenirs you bought
- how much the holiday cost altogether
- if you would recommend it to someone else
  etc.

When you are both ready, you can start. You begin and can say:

You've been on holiday, have you?

Half a crossword

The crossword below is only half filled in. Student A also has a crossword that is only half filled in. Take it in turns to ask what the missing words are, e.g. *What's 1 Down?* and answer by trying to explain each word.

Before you start, make sure you know what the following words mean:

annual	choir	pregnant
athletics	election	rice
balloon	exhausted	stare
bucket	garlic	surgeon
canal	mean	tortoise

Looking for a job (1)

You are looking for a tutor for your 10-year-old son, Jonathan, during a summer cruise with friends among the Greek islands. The person must be between twenty-two and thirty, able to swim, have a lively personality and experience in teaching children. The person will also be expected to take part in the social life on board the yacht and help with the cooking.

The job is from 14 July to 31 August and you will pay £50 a week pocket money since all food, drink, accommodation, entertainment, etc. will be free.

You have put an advertisement in the newspaper for a tutor. Student A phones up about it. If you think he/she sounds interesting, arrange a time to see him/her. (But you are only free at weekends.)

Looking for a job (2)

Situations Vacant

Baby-sitter required, one evening per week. Suit boy or girl at school.
Phone: 071-326 1008

Elderly gentleman convalescing after serious operation requires housekeeper with nursing experience. Daily help in house. Live in.
Phone: Battle 365281

You are a schoolgirl/schoolboy and are looking for a job in the evenings – possibly as a baby-sitter. You have done this before many times for your sister and friends of the family. You do not really mind which evenings you work, but would prefer Fridays. You can do it every week except for three weeks in July when you are going on holiday.

You would expect to get paid £10 a night up until 12 o'clock and £15 if later than this. You would also expect something to eat and a taxi to and from your home.

You see the above advertisement in the newspaper and decide to phone up about it. Student A is the person looking for a baby-sitter.

You can begin like this:

> Good (*evening*). I'm phoning up about the job as a baby-sitter.

33   Asking for information about a town

You are thinking of having a holiday in Hastings and phone up the Tourist and Recreation Department for further details about the town. Student A works at the above department.

Before starting, work out the type of information you require and the sort of questions you are going to ask.

For example:

–	climate	What's the weather like in July?
–	population	How many people live in Hastings?
–	accommodation	Are there any nice hotels there?
–	sports facilities	Can I play golf there?

When you are ready, you can begin like this:

> Good (*morning*). I'm thinking of having a holiday in Hastings this summer. I wonder if you could tell me something about the town?

34   Asking for information about summer language courses

You work for Summer Language Courses – an organization which arranges language courses in England during the summer. Student A phones you up for information about your courses. Answer his/her questions with the help of the information in the table. (Read through it before starting.)

SUMMER LANGUAGE COURSES

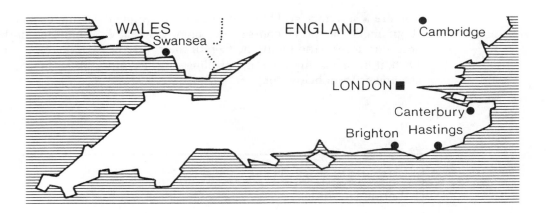

Course centres:	Cambridge, Canterbury, Hastings, Brighton and Swansea.
Course length:	Three weeks, four weeks or six weeks.
Dates:	Courses from May to September.
Tuition:	Thirty-two lessons per week, Mon–Fri. Native-speaking English teachers. Groups no larger than fifteen students.
Accommodation:	Students stay with specially selected host families and have breakfast and an evening meal every day.
Social arrangements:	Organized sports activities, excursions and evening entertainment. Each centre has its own disco and students' club.
Excursions:	Free excursions (Cambridge, Canterbury and Brighton only): London sightseeing, London shopping, London theatre visit, Windsor Safari Park. Optional excursions: weekend in Paris (for students staying in Hastings or Brighton); weekend in Ireland (for students staying in Swansea).
Travel arrangements:	Plane to Heathrow, train to course centre.
Price (including travel):	Three week course £700 Four week course £850 Six week course £1,100

35   Enrolling for an English course

You are a secretary at The English Institute. Student A phones you up about one of the special courses starting next week. Give him/her all the necessary information with the help of the course programme opposite. Then, if he/she is interested in enrolling for the course, fill in the course enrolment form below for him.

THE ENGLISH INSTITUTE

Enrolment form

Course number : . . . .

Course: . . . .

Day(s): . . . . Time: . . . .

Surname:	Christian name:
Address:	
Telephone:	

BUSINESS ENGLISH £120

A course for business executives or students in all departments of commerce and industry. Emphasis on general business needs.

Four week course. Twelve meetings. Each meeting two hours.

30931	C. Cook	Tues/Wed/Fri	09.30
30932	D. Gale	Mon/Tues/Thu	15.00
30933	C. Cook	Mon/Tues/Wed	13.00

MEDICAL ENGLISH £150

A course for doctors, nurses and others in the field of medicine who wish to learn medical terminology and practise it in discussion.

Five week course. Fifteen meetings. Each meeting three hours.

30934	P. Bull	Mon/Wed/Fri	13.00

BANKING ENGLISH £90

A special course for cashiers.

Six week course. Twelve meetings. Each meeting three hours.

30935	J. Cash	Mon	09.30
30936	J. Cash	Wed	15.30
30937	P. Money	Fri	10.00

TOURIST ENGLISH £75

A course for those visiting England.

Two week course. Ten meetings. Each meeting two hours.

30938	L. Rees	Mon–Fri	09.30
30939	L. Rees	Mon–Fri	15.00

CAMBRIDGE EXAMINATION COURSES

First Certificate £350

Eight week course.
Twenty-four meetings.
Each meeting three hours.

30940	P. Rice	Mon/Tues/Thu	09.00
30941	C. Gibbs	Mon/Wed/Fri	13.30

Cambridge Proficiency £500

Ten week course. Twenty meetings. Each meeting four hours.

30942	T. Hall	Mon/Wed	09.30
30943	P. Rice	Wed/Fri	13.30

LOOKING AT BRITAIN £100

This course looks at different aspects of life in Britain. How does an Englishman live, work and play? What is it like to live there today? What changes are taking place? Course uses B.B.C. film 'Looking at Britain'.

Eight week course. Eight meetings. Each meeting two hours.

30944	A. Long	Mon	13.30
30945	A. Long	Wed	09.30
30946	A. Long	Thu	15.00

36

One-sided dialogue: arranging an interview with 'Rubber'

Read the following dialogue with Student A.

You are a reporter for the magazine *Pop World* and would like to interview the famous Swedish group, RUBBER, who are touring England at the moment. You phone up their manager, 'Sticky' Hansen, to try to arrange a suitable day and time for the interview. Student A is 'Sticky' Hansen. Unfortunately, you can only see your part of the dialogue, so you will have to listen very carefully to what Student A says. Use the diary on the page opposite.

Before starting, read through your part to get an idea of what the dialogue is all about.

Student A: ......

You: Oh, good morning, *Mr/Miss* Hansen. This is ..... (*say your name and the magazine you work for*). I wonder if it would be possible to interview RUBBER some time next week?

Student A: ......

You: ...... (*suggest Thursday*).

Student A: ......

You: ...... (*suggest a time in the morning*).

Student A: ......

You: Yes, certainly.
(*a slight pause*)

Student A: ......

You: Yes?

Student A: ......

You: ...... (*repeat day and look at your diary*). No, I'm afraid I can't on ...... (*say day*). I've got to ...... (*explain what you have to do*).

Student A: ......

You: Er ... let me see ... (*look at diary and say, for example, Monday afternoon.*)

Student A: ......

You: Well, what about ...... (*suggest a time*)?

Student A: ......

You: ...... (*say your name. Spell it, if necessary*).

Student A: ......

You: Yes, if that's all right with you?

Student A: ......

You: Oh, good. Well, thank you very much, *Mr/Miss* Hansen, and I look forward to seeing RUBBER on ...... (*say day*). Good-bye and good luck with tonight's concert.

Student A: ......

Your diary for next week

5   Monday
 	
10.15 am. Interview lead
           Singer with '15 m.p.h.'
FREE p.m.
	9 Friday
	8.30 a.m. Dentist
	10.15 a.m. Meet Bob Wilde to
	discuss this week's edition of
	               POP WORLD

6   Tuesday
9.00 am. Drive to Brighton
1.pm. Talk to organisers
    of Brighton Pop Festival
	10 Saturday
	
	Brighton for Pop Festival
	        (all day)

7 Wednesday FREE	11 Sunday Brighton / Pop Festival (all day)
8 Thursday FREE a.m. 2 p.m. Guest on B.B.C. 'The Jimmy Old Show'	

Booking a holiday

```
┌─────────────────────────────────────────┐
│                                           │
│   SUNSHINE TOURING                        │
│   Last-minute cancellations!              │
│   Reduced prices to:                      │
│                                           │
│        Majorca      Rome                  │
│        Athens       Rhodes                │
│        Crete        Barcelona             │
│        Paris        Oslo                  │
│                                           │
│   Ring for further details                │
│   immediately!                            │
│   SUNSHINE TOURING 212 4695               │
│                                           │
└─────────────────────────────────────────┘
```

Today is Saturday. You have a two-week holiday starting on Monday. You had planned to stay at home but the weather has been so bad lately that you think it would be nice to go abroad.

You see the above advertisement in the morning paper and decide to phone up and book one of the holidays – you don't really care where you go.

Student A works for Sunshine Touring.

Before starting, have a pen ready to make a note of the following:

Destination:	....
Number of days:	....
Day of departure:	....
Time of departure:	....
Flight number:	....
Hotel:	....
Price:	....

You can begin like this:

Good (*morning*). I'm phoning about your advertisement in this morning's paper.

Fill in the missing information (3)

By asking Student A questions, fill in the missing information in the
application form below. (Student A will also ask you questions.)

APPLICATION FORM   Job applied for: ....

Name: ...... JULIE EVANS ....

Address: ....   Tel: **327497**

Age: ....**30**....   single ☐ married ☐

Education: School: .... HOVE COMPREHENSIVE ....

   College/University: ....

Qualifications: School: .... 7 O-LEVELS, 1 A-LEVEL ....

    College/University: ..... CERTIFICATE OF BUSINESS STUDIES

Present job: ....   Salary: *£15,000*

Previous jobs (state number of years and start with most recent):

.... SALES MANAGER AT SUFFOLK CHEMICALS (   )...

.... (2 YEARS)

Foreign languages spoken:

French ☒   German ☒   Italian ☐   Spanish ☐   Others: ....

Reasons for leaving present job: ....

....

....

....

Date: JANUARY 14ᵗʰ 19...   Signature: ..... Julie Evans

When you have finished, compare books to check that you have filled
in the missing information correctly.

Note to teacher on optional activities

The following two activities are included as *optional* extras rather than forming part of the main book since it was felt that they would not be appropriate for all students. Basically, these activities are examples of what can be termed 'oral jigsaw reading'; that is, where a text, a dialogue, etc. has been cut up and rearranged out of sequence. Each student is then given half the pieces and by working together they try to re-form the whole. But they must do this orally; they are not allowed to show one another their pieces of the text, dialogue, etc.

This is a very useful language activity since it not only tests the students' comprehension but is also a useful communicative activity which practises a number of language functions. For example:

- asking for things to be repeated. (Could you read that bit again, please?)
- agreeing/disagreeing. (No, I don't think that goes next./Yes, that goes next.)
- suggesting. (Why don't you read out the bits you have left?/Let's read it through again from the beginning, shall we?)
- making logical deductions. (This must be the next bit./That can't come next. There's something missing.)
    etc.

Teaching hints

1. As in all the other activities in the book students work in pairs facing one another with some sort of screen between them to avoid seeing one another's books.

2. Since the instructions for the two activities are the same in both students' books, the teacher should make sure that the students understand what they have to do by going through the instructions with the whole class before the students begin the activity.

3. Once the students understand what they should do, the teacher should leave them to do it and should at all costs avoid the temptation to step in and offer help or suggestions on how to solve the problem.

4. Once everyone has finished, the teacher can check that the activity has been completed correctly by asking one pair to read out the text, dialogue, etc. in sequence.

5. It is often worth having a short discussion about each activity afterwards to find out what the students found difficult and in particular to see whether there was anything they wished to say but did not know how to say it.

Sort it out: two letters

The following jumbled-up pieces of writing are from two letters. Unfortunately, you have only got half the pieces. Student A has the other half. Working together, try to sort out both letters. You must not show your pieces to Student A, but you can read them out. You begin. Together, mark the first letter 1–6 and the second one a–h. When you have finished, check by reading the letters out loud. (The first bit of one letter is marked.)

1.

Dear Mr and Mrs Rowley,

Thank you very much for your last letter. It was lovely to hear from you again and to hear that everyone is well. It was

Give our regards to your parents and we really look forward to seeing you in July.

With fondest wishes,

Paul & Jan

our new neighbours – they're a Mr and Mrs Grove from Leeds. They seem very nice indeed. (They've also got a 19-year-old son!)
Anyway, Anna, I'd better

Please write soon to let me know if it's all right to stay with you and please give my love to everyone – especially

it would be if you and the other students we had last year could come back again this summer. So she was thrilled when I showed her your letter!
If you can let us know

By the way, we've got five cats now. Freda had two kittens about six weeks ago. We were going to get rid of them but you know Jan – she couldn't bear the thought of giving them away

is to ask whether it would be possible to stay with you, as I enjoyed myself so much last year.
I shall be coming for two weeks – from 15 July to 30 July. (Just in

40

Sort it out: a dialogue

The following jumbled-up sentences are from a dialogue where a Mr/ Mrs Simpson, an American artist, is met at an Underground station in London by a Mr/Miss Jenkins, who works for a gallery where Mr/Mrs Simpson is having an exhibition. Unfortunately, you have only got Mr/Mrs Simpson's part. Student A has Mr/Miss Jenkins's part. Working together, try to sort out the dialogue. You must not show your part to Student A, but you can read out the sentences. Together, mark the dialogue 1–16. (Your part will be marked 2, 4, 6 etc.)

When you have finished, check by reading the dialogue out loud. Student A starts the dialogue.

Yes, very good indeed, thank you. It's a really great plane you and the French have, you know.

You lead on, Pat. I'm right behind you.

No, as a matter of fact it was my third. But every time I fly by Concorde it feels just like the first time. Don't you agree, Mr/Miss Jenkins?

Yes, that's right.

Yes, you can say that again. Is it always so busy in London?

You haven't? Well, you must try the Concorde next time. You really must. It's an experience never to be forgotten.

How do you do, Mr/Miss Jenkins. It was kind of you to meet me.

Yes, of course. Thank you. And please call me Viv. Everyone else does.